THE ALL NEW STYLE OF MAGAZINE-BOOKS

SDMLIVE®

www.SDMLIVE.com

MP

MOCY PUBLISHING
WWW.MOCYPUBLISHING.COM

Printed by CreateSpace, An Amazon.com Company

Katrina Carson

180 of my Life

ALL NEW EPISODE COMING SOON!

SDM LIVE®   amazon Prime   ROKU

SDM LIVE®

EDITOR-IN-CHIEF
D. "Casino" Bailey
casino@sdmlive.com

EDITORIAL DIRECTOR
Sheree Cranford
sheree@sdmlive.com

GRAPHIC/WEB DESIGNER
D. "Casino" Bailey
casino@sdmlive.com

ACCOUNT EXECUTIVE
Frank Harvest Jr.
frank@sdmlive.com

PHOTOGRAPHERS
Anterlon Terrell Fritz
Treagen Colston
Terance Drake

CONTRIBUTORS
April Smiley
Courtney Benjamin

COPY ORDERS & ADVERTISING OFFICE
Send Money Order or Check to:
Mocy Publishing
P.O. Box 35195
Detroit, Michigan 48235
(833) 736-5483
advertise@sdmlive.com

Copy Order Item
SDM Live Magazine Issue #19
S&H Plus Retail Price - $9.99 per copy

WWW.SDMLIVE.COM

Printed by CreateSpace, An Amazon.com Company

MP
MOCY PUBLISHING

REAL MUSIC. *Real Entertainment*
SDM LIVE
ISSUE #19
NEW

Also
K.O.
DUBMUZIK
CROWDFREAK
KING RENIGAD
KADDY REBOS

CARDI B.
THE FEMALES ARE NOW BACK ON TOP OF THE CHARTS WITH HIT MUSIC

BUNNIE
LAUNCHING AN ALL NEW TALK SHOW ON THE SDM NETWORK

WWW.SDMLIVE.COM

ISSUE 19 - 2018
CONTENTS

pg. 12
DUB MUZIK
Getting over one millon views on YouTube with his smash hit single.

pg. 16
BUNNIE MAE
Launching a new TV talk show, hitting the red carpet and more.

pg. 21
ROYALTY GANG RECORDS
All new showcase featuring the hottest new artist in the midwest.

pg. 23
TOP 10 CHARTS
The hottest albums and digital singles this month features Cardi B., Katrina Carson, Lil Dicky and more.

1

**Amazon - Fire TV Stick with
Alexa Voice Remote - Black**
$39.99
www.bestbuy.com

2

**Arlo - Pro 4-Camera Indoor/Outdoor
Wireless 720p Security Camera
System - White**
$549.99
www.bestbuy.com

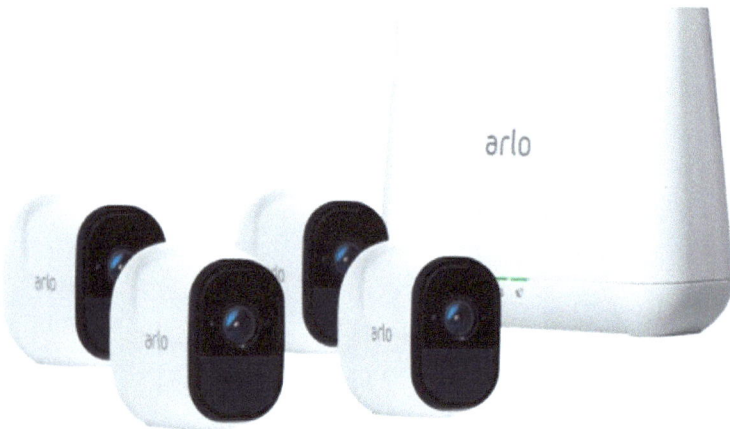

3

**Samsung - 65" Class - LED - Q6F
Series - 2160p - Smart - 4K UHD TV
with HDR**
$2099.99
www.bestbuy.com

MOCY MUSIC AND C'CLICHE
PRESENTS
SDM LIVE
2018
AWARDS
AUGUST 18, 2018
6PM-12AM
MARYGROVE COLLEGE
8425 W MCNICHOLS RD, DETROIT, MI 48221
VOTE FOR NOMINEES @ WWW.SDMLIVE.COM/VOTE

Black Comic Makes a Big Hit

WITH OVER ONE BILLON DOLLARS IN SELLS AT THE BOX OFFICE
THE MARVEL MOVIE BLACK PANTHER IS EVOLVING THE MOVIE BUSINESS.
by Cheraee C.

If you haven't been to your local movie theater yet or your neighborhood bootleg man to see Black Panther, you're missing an adventure. Whether you are into Marvel and DC movies or you just enjoy a good, action packed film, this movie is a must-see. The release of this movie was like a holiday, and there was black pride everywhere, red carpets everywhere, private screenings everywhere, and consumers were coming out dressed up in African apparel or there Sunday's best. Black Panther exemplifies black history and black culture as a lot of African Americans contributed to this successful project. Thus far, this movie has made over 1 billion dollars worldwide and is forever going to be a historical milestone. It's surpassing many other major films, challenging studio filmmaking, and the exhibition business of North America. It's nothing like a game-changer.

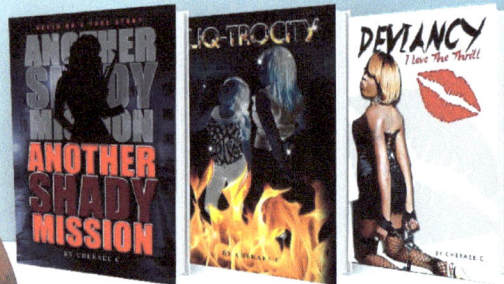

COMING SOON!!!

SDM Live
Summer Jams '18
JUNE 30, 2018
Bullfrog Bar&Grill
15414 TELEGRAPH RD REDFORD, MI 48239
9PM-2AM
TO HOST OR PERFORM
INBOX : 🅵 DONELE BAILEY | 🅵 SHEREE CHERAEE CRANFORD
EMAIL : SOSYREE@GMAIL.COM
DESIGN BY 10TAURUS GRAPHIX

Get Your Tickets Now
www.SDMLive.com

Meet the Producer

DUB MUZIK GAINS OVER ONE MILLION VIEWS ON YOUTUBE WITH HIS SMASH NEW HIT "MAN ON A MISSION" ALSO AVAILABLE ON ITUNES

by Cheraee C.

Dubmuzik is one of Detroit's top rated producers/engineer on the rise. Dubmuzik has worked with some of Detroits hottest artist Such as D12, Royce 59, Robert Curry of Day 26, Seven the General, Rock Bottom Entertainment, Lodge Boys and David McMurray of was not was as well as a host of great Artist based outta Michigan.

Going back to August 2017 Dubmuzik hit hard with his music producing career by working with Lazarus an up and coming rapper out of Detroit Michigan whom is not only a rapper of Pakistani descent he is also a Doctor.

Dubmuzik recently produced his first single off the album Music is my Medicine, titled "Man on a Mission" that currently has 1.4 million views and counting which you can fine it on YouTube. Dubmuzik is now gearing up to drop his first official Mixtape January 30th 2018 titled "No Parachute", which will feature some of Detroit top elite rappers and up and coming artists.

No Parachute will be released on all social media outlets Jan 30th 2018 Follow Dubmuzik on Instagram, Twitter, Youtube.

Instagram – @Dubmuzik313
Twitter-@Dubmuzik313
Youtube -@Dubmuzikakathealien
Email – Dubmuzik@gmail.com
Booking info – Kamillion1038@gmail.com

K.O. aka Michael Myers

THE RAPPER THAT CALLS HIMSELF MICHAEL MYERS IS KILLING THE GAME LIKE A HALLOWEEN MOVIE AND CREATING AN UNSTOPPABLE MOVEMENT
by Cheraee C.

Q. Why do you call yourself the Lyrical Michael Myers?
A. I go by the name Michael Myers cause Halloween is my favorite horror movie. I love horror flicks and I'm a big fan of Michael Myers and he always killing shit, he's unstoppable, and he always come back so I put the lyrical in front of Michael Myers to give it that creative pop cause I'm always killing shit lyrically.

Q. Does all the media attention your hometown gets affect your music?
A. No, not all. I feel like that's just more fuel for the fire in me. It's a whole another avenue of topics that only a person from Chicago can relate to. It gives me more passion, and more ideas and I think it's a big help for anyone coming out of Chicago so big s/o to my city by the way.

Q. How do you feel about other artists from your town on the rise? Do you think Chicago artists are unappreciated in the music scene?
A. I feel like it's 50/50 on that level for Chicago artists. It's a lot of upcoming rappers in my city that just need to go sit the fuck down somewhere. I love my city make no mistakes about it. I'm Chicago crazy! Westside born and raised and I'm still here, but it's a lotta niggas just gangbanging through their music in our city and that's not music to me. I can see a few songs here and there, but every song come on now and half of them end up dead anyway so it's kind of pointless. All they doing is dying behind that nonsense and exposing themselves to the police. Then on the other hand you got up and coming artists like myself that's been standing and should have been on a long time ago that's been writing, producing, recording, promoting, investing, and have great talent, and great messages in their music. Big s/o to those artists, keep pushing, we almost there yo!

Q. What would you do if you had to stop doing music?
A. I can't even answer that question. Music is the air to my lungs and the beat to my heart so I probably would just die.

Founder and CEO, Curtis Lamar

CROWDFREAK IS SEEMING TO BECOME ONE OF THE MUSIC INDUSTRIES FIRM LEADERS IN ARTIST DEVELOPMENT RELATIONS IN THE MIDWEST.

by: No'el.

Q: What up Curtis, it's cool that we finally get the opptunity to sit down and dicuss your brand. Also thanks for being here and giving SDMLive Magazine, the insite on CrowdFreak.

A: Hey, no problem! I appreciate the opportunity! I definitely wanted to give a pretty indepth perspective on my company and what it means to the upcoming artist. Thanks for giving me the opportunity and having me here!

Q: For the readers, tell us more in depth about CrowdFreak and the music artist you manage.

A: Well, the origin of Crowdfreak starts with the artist I manage, so let's start there! I started managing an artist named Quincy Banks a few years back and the first thing I wanted to attack with his artistry was performing live. Quincy had a very unique sound and I thought this would be brought to life through performing live. Being new to managing in the music industry I thought it would be easy finding shows through a simple google search. I was completely wrong! Unless you know just the right place to go to on social media or on the web, it's quite frankly impossible to find performance opportunities on showcases and/or concerts. Shortly after that I met Mauri Corey, who was a very talented artist that had good following and he had the uncanny ability to tell a story in his music. Once again, someone who I wanted to get in front of a crowd. So, I decided to start throwing my own showcases and found that finding other artist to perform and bring crowds was another issue that I was coming across. I then decided to create a website that combatted both side of the performance where promoters are able to post performance opportunities and artist are able to grab these opportunities to gain exposure in front of their selected crowd! And with the help of Myles Xdope (another artist I manage) we began to throw hugh events, giving many detroit area artist the opportunity to perform in front of great crowds!

Also CrowdFreak.com is the Ebay of performing! Artist at all walks of life, rather you're just beginning or a veteran in music, are able to log onto our site and search performance opportunities in their area and grab a slots to perform instantly. There are no hidden fees and it provides instant access to stage! Vice versa, as a promoter or venue, you're able to post performance slots and connect with artist in a way like never before! Our ultimate goal is to be the missing link between the performer and the performance!

Q: Elaborating on the process, how can music artist sign up for CrowdFreak events? And how is it beneficial?

A: Its pretty simple to sign-up! All aspiring musicians can go to crowdfreak.com and create an account which takes less than 2 minutes. Once logged in they can begin to explore performance opportunities and lock in their first performance!

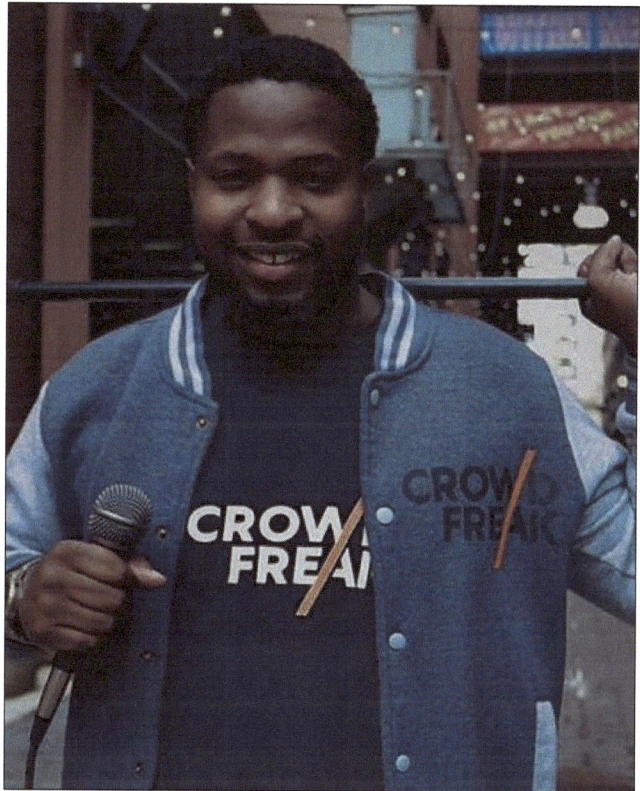

Its beneficial because it gives artist direct access to the stage! We have given out opportunities for artist to open for national acts like, Gucci mane, Kap G, Taylor Gang, 21 savage, Jacquees and more! Opportunities that otherwise would be impossible to find!

Q: Could you share an experience in which you planned the development of one of your CrowdFreak programs and effectively maintain favorable public perception of the event?

A: This summer was amazing! We threw several concert w/ acts such as, Taylor Gang, Kap G, Og Maco, and Lil Debbie and the amazing part about it was the opportunities we gave to upcoming artist in detroit. We gave over 30+ artist the opportunity to perform at these epic concerts and it was overall a very satisfying feeling to do so! Since then we have been consistent with our services and we have received nothing but positive feedback!

Q: With the current success of your brand and the presentational showcases you conduct, what can the music industry expect from CrowdFreak in the future?

A: Now if i give you all the secrets, what will make Crowdfreak unique lol No but, just know CrowdFreak.com will be a one stop shop for everything music in the foreseeable future.

Having Brunch with Bunnie

LIGHTS, CAMERA, ACTION!!! ALL NEW ENTERTAINMENT SHOW COMING TO THE SDM TELEVISION NETWORK THIS SPRING

by Cheraee C.

Q. What do you enjoy most about being in the entertainment industry and why?
A. I enjoy all the characters and personalities that I get to meet! I enjoy being able to learn their story and giving them a positive platform to showcase them and their talent/business.

Q. What exactly do you do in the industry and what is your entertainment name?
A. My entertainment name is Bunnie Mae or Bunnie the Blogger, but I prefer Bunnie. Whew! I have so many hats! I am a Red Carpet Host/Media Correspondent/Socialite and soon to be Talk Show Host.

Q. How and when are you going to be a talk show host?
A. I will be hosting my show "Brunch With Bunnie" on the SDM Network! It will basically be my blog elevated! A positive, enjoyable environment for people to showcase and hopefully have a few laughs! I don't want to spill all the beans, but make sure you hop on The Bunnie Hole Media FB page to check for updates!

Q. What is your favorite topic to blog about? How can people read your blog?
A. Anything positive! I think my favorite topic in blogging is #BadBunnieAlert where we highlight a successful entrepreneur! Our website is being revamped right now to include our Red Carpet Hosting where you'll be able to book the red carpet experience. But in the meantime you can follow us on FB: The Bunnie Hole or IG: BunnietheBlogger and Twitter: The Bunnie Hole.

Q. Have you seen any of the shows on SDM Live Network?
If so, which show/shows can you relate to and why?
A. I just recently became familiar with the SDM Live Network, so I can't say that I have favorite. I really enjoy all of the ones I have been able to view, but Hilltop Gospel was great, I haven't seen it in a while though.

Q. What is the craziest thing you've seen being on the red carpet?
A. Well, I have seen quite a few things on the Red Carpet! I think the craziest thing was probably when we covered an event that Safaree was at. There were adult entertainers on the Red Carpet! It was so much fun and very entertaining!

Q. Out of all the celebrities you've met on or before the Red Carpet, which celebrity or celebrities inspired you the most?

A. I think the most inspiring celebrity that I met was actually before the Red Carpet, when I was just blogging. I have two actually and my first was Keke Wyatt. She inspired me so much because she always perseveres. Through so much controversy that has come her way along with still maintaining her family life, it's all so inspirational. Another of my favorite is Pilar Scratch, celebrity stylist and mogul. She gave me my first magazine feature and always is so encouraging and positive. She let's me know that anything is possible with a little hard work!

Q. What are your hobbies when you're not blogging or on the Red Carpet?

A. I love spending time with my family! I also love to travel and I have a few trips planned this year already! I'm an avid reader so I'm constantly on the lookout for new materials to read!

Q. What is the next Red Carpet event you have coming up or is it strictly confidential?

A. Most of my events are not confidential. I love for people to come out and show support! My next Red Carpet Event is April 21, 2018 for Revenge Cosmetics "Pretty Faces & Fashion Show" at the Livonia Commerce Center from 2pm-6pm! You can contact me or Revenge Cosmetics for more information regarding tickets!

The Return of Cassette Tapes

HOW MANY MUSIC FANS ARE BRINGING BACK VINTAGE CASSETTE TAPES

by Semaja Turner

Just when the world thought that music streaming was going to take over the music industry indefinitely, the tables have turned. Reports say that Apple will be taking music downloads from the iTunes store by early 2019 and Amazon Music has stopped supporting mp3 imports. Also, Target and Best Buy are reportedly going to stop selling CDs by the summer time. In 2017, vinyl record sales accounted for 14% of all physical albums purchases and cassette tape sales have risen. In the UK and the US, cassette sales have been skyrocketing and growth is only expected to continue. Apparently, recent albums from Lana Del Rey, Jay-Z, and Taylor Swift as well as films such as Guardians of The Galaxy 2 have led to the cassette revival.

Just when we probably thought cassette tapes were nonexistent or we were never going to see them again, we were wrong. It's never a dull moment in the music industry and anything can make a comeback including cassette tapes.

SNICK CAPONE

IG: @SNICKTHEBOSS

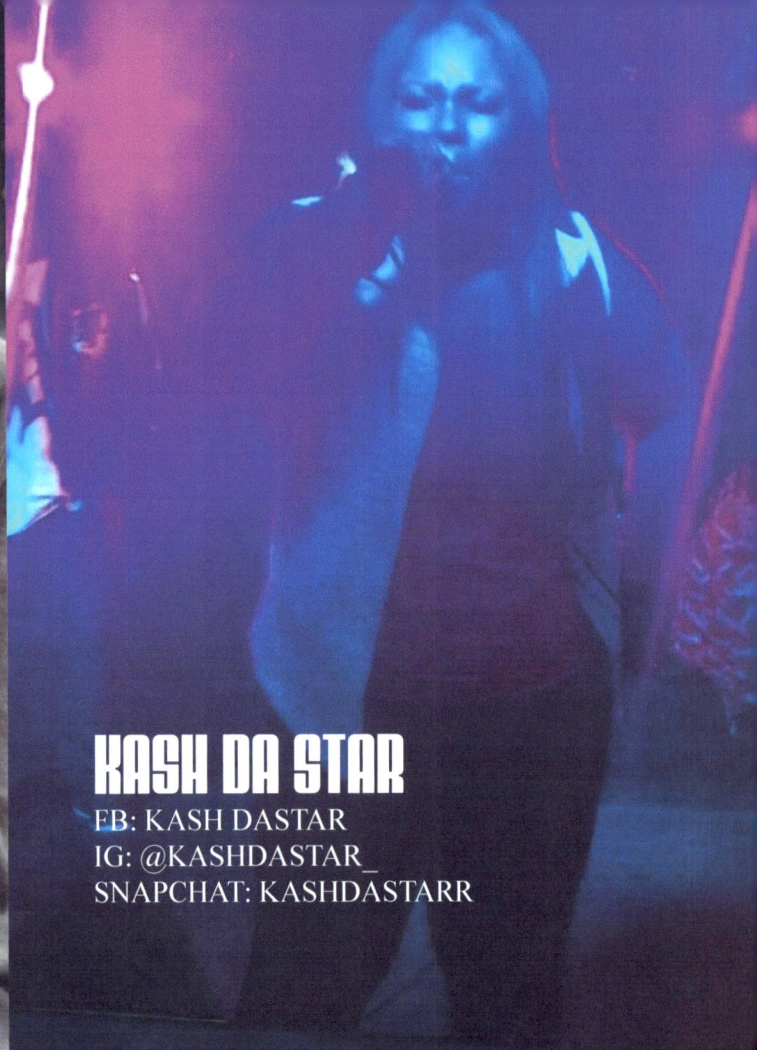

KASH DA STAR

FB: KASH DASTAR
IG: @KASHDASTAR_
SNAPCHAT: KASHDASTARR

DUB SACK D GREATTT

IG:DUBSACKDGREATTT
FB:DUBSACKDGREATTT
TWITTER:DUBSACKDGREATTT

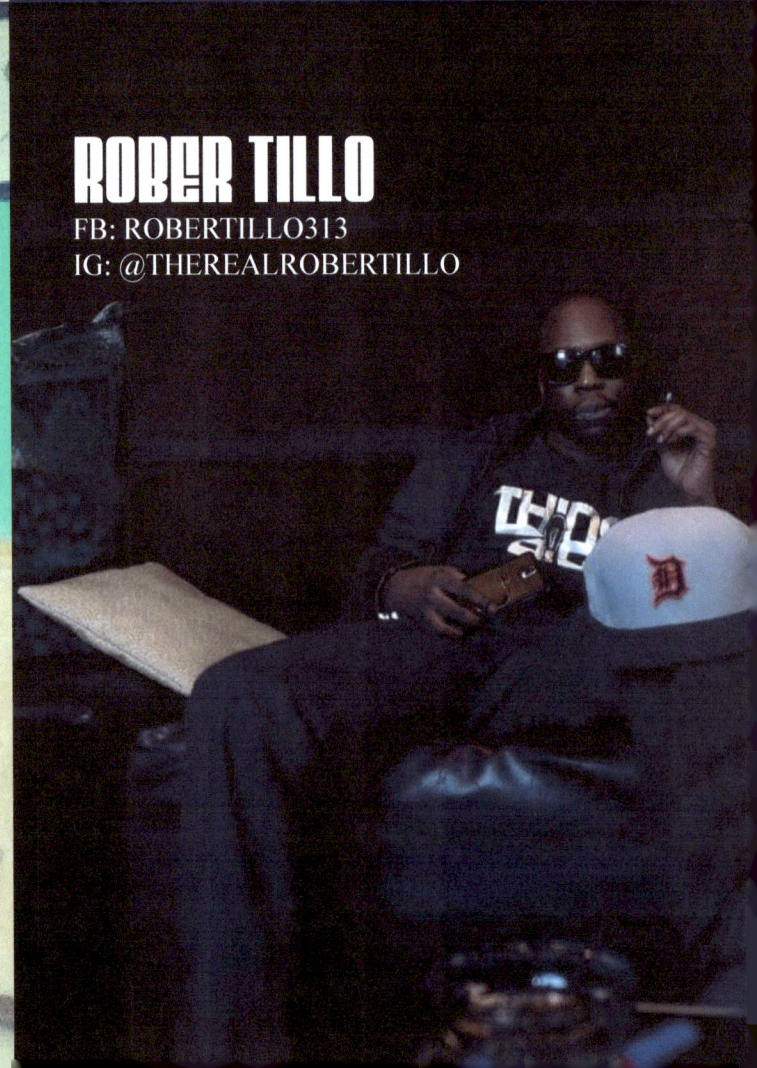

ROBER TILLO

FB: ROBERTILLO313
IG: @THEREALROBERTILLO

JASON SMITH
FB: JASON SMITH

RAZEAL
FB: ARNETTA LOVESMESSIAH GRABLE
IG: @ARIESPRINCESS

GENTRY PITTS
B: GENTRY PITTS
G: YOU_KNOW_THAT_ITS_PITTS
YOUKNOWTHATITSPITTS
WITTER: GPITTS1988

ROYALTY GANG RECORDS SHOWCASE

iEventTixx®

BUY TICKETS. SELL TICKETS. GET PAID INSTANTLY.

The only Event website were Sellers can split the payout per ticket sold up to 5 Paypal accounts and get paid instantly.

www.iEventTixx.com

TOP 10 CHARTS

TOP 10 DIGITAL SINGLES AND ALBUMS
MAY 1, 2018

TOP 10 CHARTS

CARDI B WALKS THE RED CARPET IN FROST WHITE APPEARAL AT THE GRAMMYS.

TOP #1

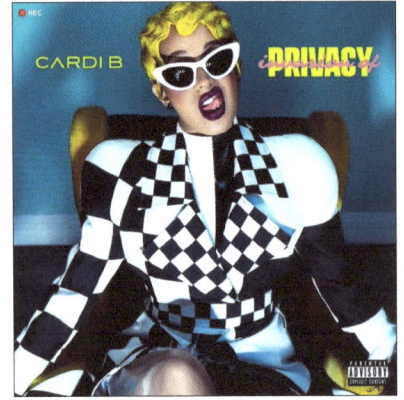

Cardi B
Invasion of Privacy

Female rap star Cardi B has one of the best albums this year with hit record "Drip".

TOP 10 SINGLES CHART OF THE MONTH

No.	Artist - Song Title
1	CARDI B - DRIP FT. MIGOS
2	DRAKE - GOD'S PLAN
3	KATRINA CARSON - AIN'T ABOUT TO WAIT FT. AKINYELE THE BLK NIGHT
4	CHRIS BROWN - TEMPO
5	LIL DICKY - FREAKY FRIDAY FT. CHRIS BROWN
6	KING DILLON - HASHTAG FT. MTR & ROZEGOLD B
7	MIGOS - WALK IT TALK IT FT. DRAKE
8	BRUNO MARS - FINESSE FT. CARDI B
9	LEON - LOOK LIKE BAE
10	H.E.R. - FOCUS

TOP 10 ALBUMS CHART OF THE MONTH

No.	Artist - Album Title
1	CARDI B - INVASION OF PRIVACY
2	ROCKY BADD - ROCKO
3	GOODBOYZ - C4
4	KATRINA CARSON - I WAS...I AM
5	MIGOS - CULTURE
6	DRAKE - MORE LIFE
7	KENDRICK LAMAR - DAMN.
8	SZA - CTRL
9	BRUNO MARS - 24K MAGIC
10	H.E.R. - H.E.R.

Rocko
ARTIST: Rocky Badd
RATING: 4

In the city of Detroit with her newest album, *Rocko*. Rocky Badd showcases her efficient rap skills and charming Rocky Badd released a music project that's combined with short tales of love, struggle, betrayal, loyalty and success vocals over a high-mid tempo production. Layed with piano keys, and drum kicks on her debut album, Rocko demonstrates the multi-liners within Rocky's verses and her diversity when it relates to her flow. While listening, we're able to learn that there's two sides to the west side music artist. Tracks such as Tenfeaturing Smokecamp Chino and The Greatest, featuring Mauri Corey depict an ebullient, chaotic flow that entices listeners, making the tracks endlessly playable and enjoyable. Other tracks such as With You, and Sweet Lady utters a more seductive, intimate effect with graceful wordplay and catchy hooks. Full of memorable lyrics with well blended features from Jeno Cashh, Cammy Bands, SAM, Smokecamp Chino, AllStar Lee, Mauri Corey, Shredgang Mone, and Tayy Dior, this properly composed fifteen track album represents a young artist strive while on the come up towards success. Don't sleep on artist when there's a multitude of potential present. Rocko is confident, cleverly written, motivational and femininely fearless! Check out Detroit's very own, Rocky Badd and her debut album, Rocko on all digital streaming services.

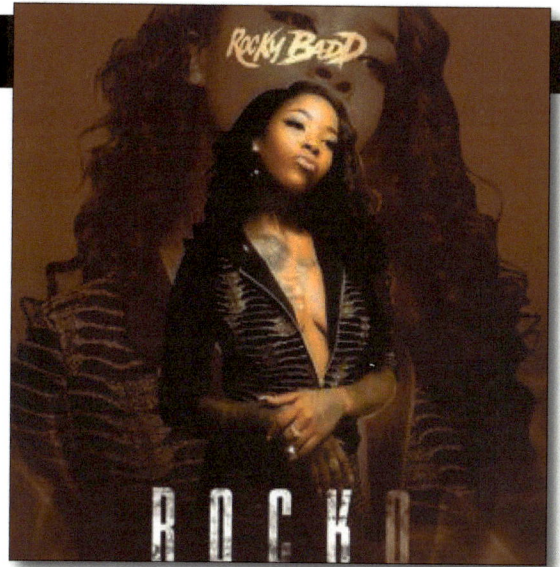

"All They See Is Pain, They Ain't Seen What I've Been Through. Give Em' All Of Me, I Ain't Rich and Don't Pretend To. Let Them Niggas Ball Baby, We Goin' Touch A Mill Soon."

C4
ARTIST: Goodboyz
RATING: 4

The young Detroit native has been truly working hard to perfect his craft as an emcee in this past year. Early November, the Goodboyz artist released his latest project; a four track EP titled "C4" in which listeners received a clear glimpse of what to expect for future projects. Mauri Corey pleases listeners with his new mixtape, City Slicker 2.

In just one month, the twenty-five year old delivered a project that presented anguish, obtaining disposable income, and separating himself from the phonies.

The production was greatly done by ill Shad, Cbsm Henny, Yung Reg, Gohard Tae, Luke Superior and Detroitredd that offered a wide variety of drum kicks, snares and rhythmic kick sequences that allows you to perceive many ascending and descending tempos throughout City Slicker 2. With features from Ava Marie, Fresh, Lil Baby, Zjaih, Yung Dash, Poppa, Yung Reg, Cbsm Henny, Quincy Banks, Yella Montanna, FA Meech, Leno 380, DC Porter, Ty Rose, Shredgang Boogz, June Taylor, FL Dinero, and Rocky Badd, Mauri Corey's aggressive tone presented numerous emotions of a strive, hunger and passion; pulling anyone down to reach the top tier in the music industy. Tracks like Too Fake, Richard Hamilton featuring Leno 380 and DC Porter, and Hate On Me featuring Fresh illustrate a confidently, truculent approach, intermixing energetic deliveries and raw lyrics creating a wonderful intonation with their versatile flows. Other tracks such as Lil Baby featuring Zjaih, and two tracks featuring Ava Marie, Cops and Toss It Up contribute a blissful turn around for the mixtape. Adding soulful early nineties samples with piercing verbiage and sharp vocals, curiosity of Ava Marie. From the intro, paying homage to Tupac Shakur's

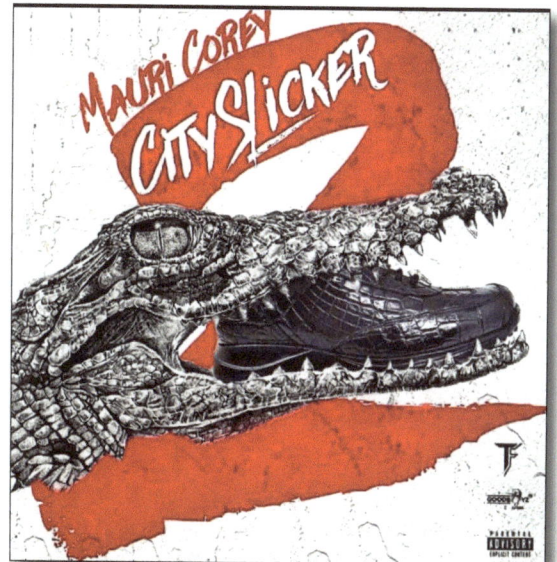

1996 classic, to incorporating fellow multifaceted Detroit artist, City Slicker 2 is lyrically fashioned from a music artist perspective of creating his own generational wealth; turning nothing into something. Go and listen to Mauri Corey's second installment of the City Slicker series on Apple Music, iTunes, Spotify, Tidal, Amazon and Youtube. "Scammin' Up Til I'm Rich and My Momma Straight. Juugin' Plays To Get Money In All Kind Of Ways. I Was Broke Had To Suffer Fore' All

HEELS &
SKILLZ

Nona Malone
is a beautiful model
from Houston, TX.

instagram
@nonamalone313

Photography by
@barearmy

HEELS &
SKILLZ

HEELS & SKILLZ

Kendra Kouture

A video and runway
model from Muskegon, MI.

instagram
@kouture_world

Cheraee's Corner

WHY DO PEOPLE GIVE UP ON THEIR DREAMS
AND BUSINESS VENTURES SO EASILY?

by Cheraee C.

Is giving up really easier then succeeding? How can we say we believe in loyalty if we are continuously being disloyal to our purposes and God given gifts? Nothing or no one should ever make you give up on your dreams or businesses. We all experience hi-cups, roadblocks, distractions, life-changing events, and etc during our individual journeys in life, but the goal is not to quit, it's to regroup, rebuild, and increase the faith.

Increase your strength, increase your wisdom, and increase your investments. If the universe keeps throwing you distractions, you have to throw something back, why not throw something positive back like an accomplishment or a blessing. People need to learn how to be thankful and comfortable with small success, before they can even encounter big success.

Clearly, if people are tired of trying and not making it, they need to evaluate themselves and their lifestyles. Just think, when a phone doesn't work, it's either broken, it's needs to be re-charged, or you didn't pay the bill, but rarely is the case a manufacture malfunction. Therefore understand there is a cost to success and if you can't handle life's punches, you are not ready to be successful.

NEXT 2 BLOW

KADDY REBOS

Q. Is music your first love or is your love for music changing?
A. I will always love music, but to a degree some music has evolved into something I sometimes don't understand, but it's good. It's good you know.

Q. How do you feel music has changed and evolved and how do you feel music is supposed to be?
A. I think the digital world has taken some of the creativity away making analog style seem dated. I like some of the direction music is going, but I feel this hippy trippy/thug movement has taken a grip on the youth. Nobody's in love anymore, women aren't celebrated as much, being careless is the feeling now. I'm a R&B guy. I like the thought of being in love, you feel me. It's different.

Q. So why don't you start a movement of your own with similar R&B artists and bring it back?
A. Hahaha. I'm tryna get my thang off the ground! This game ain't cheap. There is a group of us that connect and support each other.. Once I debut the Soul EP and get the response from the people, I'll then know what direction to go. Without you, there's no me.

Q. What things do you plan to do to get more attention and status in the music world?
A. I plan on continuing to promote myself through social media, FB, IG, and music videos. Also, continuing to perform at venues, doing the live thing.

Q. When can we expect your EP and what type of music, topics, and vibes can we expect to hear on your EP?
A. To be honest, I don't have a date, my homeboys tease me a lot. They be like 2020 Kaddy? Lol, I'm just following what the creator above gives me. There's no time limit on that you feel me. Imma just keep dropping. I got about 11 songs done, I work a job, so it's been difficult with finances a little, but I like the direction the creator has me in, it's humbling. My music is a reflection of what I've seen, how it makes me feel and hopefully allowing the listener to feel and enjoy it with me. Just gold old R&B baby.

Q.

Since it's a new year, do you have any new year resolutions planned?
A. I plan on being consistent and creating a balance between my music career and my personal life.

Q. What do you enjoy most about doing music?
A. At first it was a cry for people to hear my struggles, but I grew to love the culture of Hip Hop as a whole. I love telling stories creatively.

Q. What kind of struggles do you vent about in your music?
A. I talk about the struggle of being raised in a single mother home, fake friends, struggle to find love, being in the streets, and my dance life.

Q. Do you still dance and what's the pros and cons of managing shows versus dancing?
A. I manage shows now so I make more money with less hassle. The only con is the temptation to get back in the game.

Q. How do you end up joining forces with Loyalty Management?
A. I used to throw shows and I remember dropping off tickets to her home and we would always have business conversations so we eventually started working together.

NEXT 2 BLOW

KING RENIGAD

SNAP SHOTS

SNAP SHOTS

SNAP SHOTS

Email Your Snap Shots to
snapshots@sdmlive.com

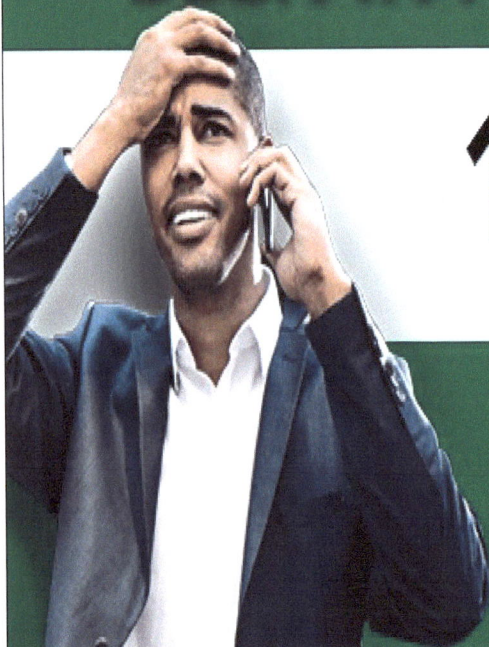

5DS PRODUCTIONS
THE PRINT MEDIA CENTER.

PRINT

DIGITAL & PRESS RUN PRICE LIST

BUSINESS CARD 2x3.5 INCHES		TRIFOLD BROCHURE 8.5x11 INCHES		POSTCARDS 4x6 INCHES	
100	$10	250	$150	250	$50
500	$20	500	$180	500	$55
1000	$30	1000	$230	1000	$65
5000	$100	5000	$350	5000	$130
10000	$170	10000	$680	10000	$250

**FLYERS - BROCHURES - BANNERS - BUSINESS CARDS - CD INSERTS
CALENDARS - EVENT TICKETS - POSTCARDS - POSTERS
YARD SIGNS - AND MUCH MORE**

DIGITAL & PRESS RUN PRINTING

FAST TURN AROUND PRINTING

GET FREE SHIPPING ON ALL ORDERS

YOU SAVE MONEY WHEN YOU PRINT AT
WWW.THEPRINTMEDIACENTER.COM
24/7 ONLINE ORDERING. CALL US NOW 1.888.718.2999

Urban Fiction, Spiritual, Motivation and more.
Order a book from Mocy Publishing today and receive FREE shipping.

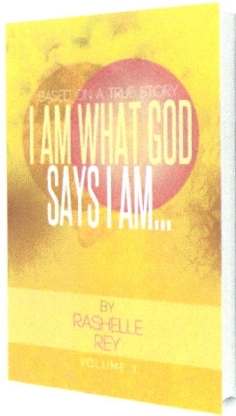

I Am What God Says I Am...
By Rashelle Rey

Item #: IAWGS29
Price: $9.99

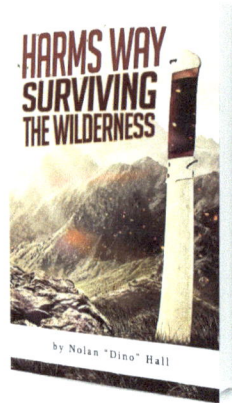

Harm's Way
By Nolan "Dino" Hall

Item #: HWS821
Price: $15.99

The Shadiest Mission Ever
By Cheraee C.

Item #: TSME28
Price: $12.99

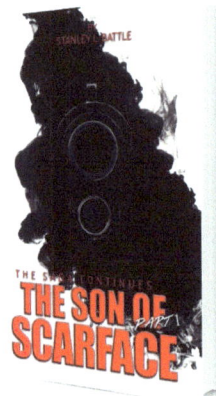

The Son Of Scarface – Part 1
By Stanley L. Battle

Item #: TSOS01
Price: $12.99

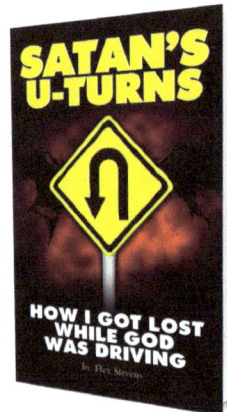

Satan's U-Turns
By Flex Stevens

Item #: SUT382
Price: $9.99

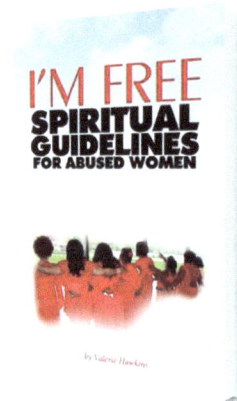

I'm Free
By Valerie Hawkins

Item #: IFTSG82
Price: $14.99

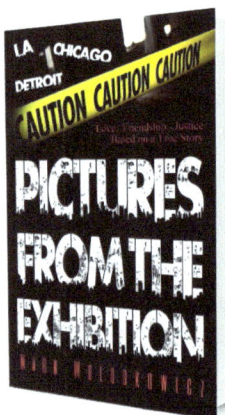

Pictures From The Exhibition
By Mark Wolodkowicz

Item #: PFAE292
Price: $15.99

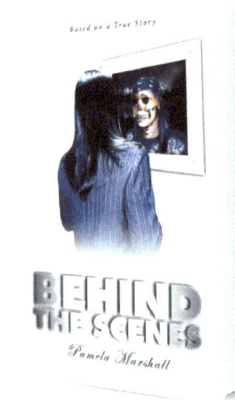

Behind The Scenes
By Pamela Marshall

Item #: BTS721
Price: $15.99

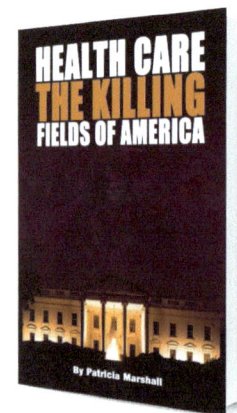

Health Care
By Patricia Marshall

Item #: HCTABF2
Price: $17.99

www.mocypublishing.com
order online and receive FREE shipping. Limit time offer.

THE ALL NEW STYLE OF MAGAZINE-BOOKS

SDM LIVE ®

www.ingramcontent.com/pod-product-compliance
Lightning Source LLC
Chambersburg PA
CBHW040018050426
42452CB00002B/38